Sitting with Seamoor

Other Books by Robert F. Wolff and Majestic Glory

UNITY: Awakening the One New Man

Have You Seen the Lamb?

My First 40 Days with the Lord

Catch & Release: A Church Set Free

Sitting with Seamoor

A Pathway to Peace

Robert F. Wolff

© Copyright 2018 — Robert F. Wolff

All rights reserved. This book is protected by the copyright laws of the United States of America. This book may not be copied or reprinted for commercial gain or profit. The use of short quotations or occasional page copying for personal use is permitted and encouraged. Permission will be granted upon request. All rights reserved worldwide. Scripture quotations are from the Tree of Life (TLV) translation of the Bible. Copyright © 2015 by The Messianic Jewish Family Bible Society. Scripture quotations are also from the New King James Version. Copyright © 1982 by Thomas Nelson, Inc. Used by permission. Also from THE HOLY BIBLE, NEW INTERNATIONAL VERSION®, NIV® Copyright © 1973, 1978, 1984, 2011 by Biblica, Inc.® Used by permission. All rights reserved worldwide. All emphasis within Scripture is the author's own.

Drawbaugh Publishing Group

444 Allen Drive
Chambersburg, PA 17202

ISBN Paperback : 978-1-941746-45-5

ISBN Ebook : 978-1-941746-46-2

For Worldwide Distribution, Printed in the United States

1 2 3 4 5 6 7 8 / 22 21 20 19 18

Endorsements

Sit back and take a pleasant journey into Kingdom truths through the eyes of young Curiosity and his sage-friend, Seamoor. Through the power of allegory, Bob presents powerful principles that are sure to encourage and strengthen the new believer, as well as the seasoned traveler well acquainted with Kingdom pathways. An enjoyable and profitable read!

Jane Hansen Hoyt
President/CEO
Aglow International

Sitting with Seamoor is just delightful! It will make you more curious and help you to see more about the One New Man in Yeshua/Jesus who is so crucial for our times.

Grant Berry, Author
Founder/President
Messiah's House and Reconnecting Ministries

Bob Wolff writes with a whimsical creativity that belies the serious and powerful truths of his subject matter. We are drawn into the conversations between Curiosity and Seamoor and find there our own questions of faith as well as our own faith questioned. This book is a refreshing time spent in the presence of a trusted friend.

Peter Tsukahira
Cofounder
Carmel Congregation

Bob Wolff has a great ability to bring truth across in the most winsome ways. *Sitting with Seamoor* is a case in point. He presents Kingdom principles to set the course for our future together as Jews and Gentiles in Yeshua/Jesus.

Dan Juster
Restoration from Zion
Tikkun International

Candidly confronting the issues of the day, Bob Wolff puts forward in storybook form the perspectives of both secularists and biblical pietists. The gracious responses of the "grace-filled" and biblically savvy Seamoor to contemporary problems bring clarity and hope to those otherwise floundering at the edge of the downward pull of the cosmic whirlpool. But rescue is found by the assurances of Truth and Grace. *Sitting with Seamoor* is a good motivational and educational read for those eager to let their lights shine in a dark world.

Raymond Gannon, PhD
National Jewish Field Representative
Assemblies of God

Curiosity's Journey

Foreword ix

Befriending 1

1. Miracles – "Well then, you haven't been looking." 3
2. Keep the Book – "God's in the business of stretching." 9
3. Right and Wrong – "God always keeps His word." 15
4. Creation – "Yeshua came to take care of our mistakes." . 21
5. Patience – "God will not allow anything to be overlooked." 27
6. Our Peace – "And you're going to live to see it happen." 33
7. Leap of Faith – "You need spiritual eyes." 39

Rending 45

8. Science – "Science is never satisfied with today's answers." 47
9. Love – "How's that for real power?" 53
10. Connecting the Dots – "The stepping stones to peace." . 59
11. Walk in Unity – "Shines like light in a dark place." 65
12. Outside Thinking – "It's the internal desires that drive us." 71
13. Family – "Unity satisfies the law of attraction." 77
14. Purple Ticket – "Your ticket was paid for." 83

Never-Ending 89

15. Perfection – "Imperfect people do His perfect work." ... 91
16. Changing Direction – "The truth has a time to its telling." 97
17. Potential – "Just tell me what you see." 103
18. Walls – "The world judges our decision." 109
19. Joy – "How about a double portion?" 115
20. One New Man – "We won't find it without God." 121
21. Godly Government – "God blesses His followers." 127

Foreword

I love the way Bob is continually listening to the Lord for ways to get the message of Yeshua/Jesus to the next generations, encouraging them to follow the hunger that is within every heart. In this newest book, Bob touches on just about every question that is part of that pilgrimage—miracles, creation, resurrection, judgment, Jew-Gentile relationships, the Bible, and much more.

Seamoor is the wise sage who knows how to challenge his young friend, and Curiosity represents the eternal longing within all of us. Listen in on their conversations from week to week. Use their journey to open doors of discussion with other truth-seekers, a journey that will ultimately result in producing passionate followers of Jesus and lovers of His Word.

This is a great book to be used in small groups. Once you've sat in on the dialogue between Curiosity and Seamoor, invite your friends and family together to wrestle with these questions and gain needed insight to firmly establish our faith.

Don Finto
Pastor Emeritus, Belmont Church
President/Founder, Caleb Company

With Gratitude

Books never write themselves. They require wisdom and guidance from trusted ones.

My loving, gifted, and steadfast wife Wendy provided your warm introduction with her cover art.

My confidant Elijah Benavidez inspires me in the Spirit.

My mentor Ray Gannon encourages my every step.

My coach Dean Drawbaugh keeps me on track.

My friend Wayne Headley walked me through the concept.

My partners Don Enevoldsen and Marty Reitzen caught the vision and stood with me from the beginning.

And of course, to all those living now and forevermore whose contributions have shown me the beauty of the everlasting pathway to Yeshua.

Family, friends, and faithful ones, this book is now yours to enjoy, share, and lead us to the Lifter of our heads.

God wants to be friends with us

Befriending

Miracles

Keep the Book

Right and Wrong

Creation

Patience

Our Peace

Leap of Faith

Week One

Miracles

"Well then, you haven't been looking."

Miracles

It was a sunny day when Curiosity stumbled across Seamoor for the umpteenth time. He'd passed him on the pathway often, but hadn't paid him much heed. Seamoor was relaxing on the park bench in his usual attire—faded trousers, work shirt, and baseball cap. He looked harmless enough.

Last week, following the break in his philosophy class, Curiosity got wind of a conversation some of his classmates had with this fellow Seamoor who liked to hang out on this nearby perch. It seems Seamoor had shown great wisdom regarding how to make peace. He mentioned a character out of the Bible named "One New Man."

Curiosity didn't know about One New Man, or what this person had to do with making peace. And he'd never spoken with Seamoor. Who was this guy? If he was so smart, how could he have been around for so long without anyone paying much attention to him?

Curiosity was hooked. Questions swirled around inside his cranium. If this guy Seamoor had any insights to offer about the Creator of the universe, then Curiosity wanted to pick his brains.

Philosophy class had just ended and there sat Seamoor, so Curiosity cautiously approached, taking a seat next to him. The student decided to break the ice.

"Hi. My name's Curiosity. I hear you're in touch with God."

Seamoor's response startled him.

"**Yes. Of course. Aren't you?**"

Curiosity stammered, "Well, ummm. I'm not sure."

"**So if you're not sure, then how will you know when you are sure?**"

"I'll know," replied Curiosity, "when someone proves it to me."

"**What kind of proof do you need?**"

"I suppose a miracle would do the job."

"**There are plenty of miracles.**"

"Not that I've seen."

"**Well then, you haven't been looking.**"

"I think if there were a miracle I would notice."

"**I see. You know how to spot miracles. That's fascinating. Tell me, what do you look for?**"

Curiosity was at a loss. Deciding to test the older fellow's wisdom, he blurted out, "Someone raised from the dead!"

Seamoor chuckled. "It's already been done."

"You can't prove that."

"**I don't need to. They wrote a book about it. It's the world's best seller.**"

"That book is thousands of years old."

"**What's wrong with that?**"

"How can you tell if it's true?"

"**You said you would notice if there was a miracle.**"

"That means I need to see it."

"**So isn't a book that sells for thousands of years a miracle?**"

Curiosity was flustered. "I'm not sure."

Seamoor tilted his head toward the younger man.

"**Well that's an honest answer. But now we may have to reconsider how we recognize a miracle.**"

Curiosity shot back, "I didn't say I know how to spot every miracle."

"**No you didn't. But I thought I'd let you advise me what to look for.**"

"Yeah, I guess you're right about that. But God's invisible, so how am I going to know when I've heard or seen him?"

"**Isn't that book enough?**"

"Well, we need to test and see if it's true."

"**How about the test of time? It's passed that test with flying colors.**"

"Sure, but that doesn't tell us that what it says is true."

"**OK. You're right about that. If something is true it's best to have some personal experience to confirm our perspective.**"

"I agree. I want to have some point of reference to test things out. Otherwise it's just other people's experiences, not my own."

"**So, have you read the book?**"

"No, but I've heard about it."

"**What have you heard?**"

"I've heard that the stories are so old that you can't tell when or where, or even if they happened."

"**Interesting. Doesn't seem to have hurt its popularity.**"

"Just because it's popular doesn't make it right."

"**I have to agree with you. So what would make it right?**"

"Like I said before, I need proof."

Behind them a train whistled. As it drew near, Seamoor dusted off his trousers with his baseball hat, revealing long white hair. He was in need of a trim and a shave.

"Well then, I suppose you'll need to look inside."

With that Seamoor stood up.

"Are you leaving?"

"I'll see you next week."

With that the elder strode toward the railway station. Curiosity looked down. There on the bench was a well-worn Bible. He grabbed it and began to shout after Seamoor, but he was nowhere to be found. The train whistled its departure. Curiosity scanned up and down the empty platform. Had time just skipped? He could swear the train was just pulling into the station when he picked up the Bible. An instant later it had already left.

Curiosity's Corner

I met this guy today. He left me his Bible. It says his name is Seamoor. He's making me think about miracles. He acts like they happen all the time. I believe in miracles, but I'm not so sure. He was asking some tough questions. I like that. He seems to know what's going on inside the Bible. I've been looking for some answers. I think I'll start to read from the beginning. This could be interesting.

More from Seamoor

Isaiah 55:11

John 1:1

Jeremiah 32:27

Hebrews 13:8

Proverbs 3:19

Week Two

Keep the Book

"God's in the business of stretching."

Keep the Book

The following week, Seamoor was stationed at his regular spot. It was a little breezy, so he donned a windbreaker and a scarf. When Curiosity arrived, he was feeding the birds.

"Good afternoon, my young friend."

"How is it that you know so much?"

"It's nice to see you."

Realizing he had bypassed appropriate social graces, Curiosity settled down on the bench and took a deep breath. With a greater sense of appreciation, he responded.

"It's nice to see you too."

Seamoor nodded and continued to cast seed.

"I have all these questions I want to ask you, but I don't know where to start."

Seamoor kept on with the seed.

Curiosity suddenly remembered and grabbed his backpack. He pulled out the Bible.

"You forgot this."

"I didn't forget anything."

Curiosity had to weigh these words.

"You didn't?"

"You said you hadn't read the book."

"Wow, so you gave it to me? Or should I say you let me borrow it?"

"That depends on if you plan on reading it."

"Well I read the first chapter."

"That's excellent."

"So do you believe all this?"

"It's a lot to take in, isn't it?"

"No kidding."

"**The real question is, 'Do you believe what you're reading?'**"

"It's very interesting. I want to believe it, but it's a real stretch."

"**God's in the business of stretching.**"

Curiosity stopped talking. He could feel that last remark work its way into his being. This fellow presented something that he hadn't considered.

"**You can keep the book.**"

The remark brought Curiosity back to the reality of his present situation.

"Really? It's obvious you've used it a lot. Are you sure?"

"**I've got others at home. I was hoping you'd enjoy reading it.**"

"Gosh. Thanks. Don't know what to say."

"**Nothing to say. I'm glad you're interested.**"

"I can't stop thinking about God making the world."

"**Me neither.**"

Both started to laugh. Curiosity could feel his concerns about his new friend starting to melt. He hardly knew the man, yet there was something so warm and familiar about him. And he had given him his Bible. It was clear this book was important to him. Yet he decided to give it to someone who just met him. What a nice guy.

"Just supposing that God did make the world…"

Seamoor sat back against the bench. Curiosity looked up at the sky.

"…think of all the effort it would have taken to make all of this. I mean just how big and how smart would God have to be to figure all this out?"

Seamoor observed the younger one wrestling with his ideas.

"I have trouble believing something God made would be in such a mess."

"**How do you think God feels about that?**"

"How do you know God has feelings?"

"Well how could you make something like this if you didn't have feelings?"

"I don't rightly know. It's just all so overwhelming."

"Did you ever think it's supposed to be overwhelming?"

"What good is it to be in the middle of something you can't fully understand?"

"Good question."

"My mind isn't big enough to figure all of this out."

"It's not supposed to be."

"But the book says, '*So God created man in His own image.*'"

"So you studied the first chapter?"

"Well sort of. But I heard that before."

"Do you accept that God made you in his image?"

"I'm not sure. This is about everyone, not just me."

Seamoor arose.

"We are man. We are woman. We are human. We are humanity. And everyone of us is made in God's image."

"If we're all made in God's image, why don't we get along with each other?"

"Some people get along better than others."

"We should all take care of each other, but we don't."

"Not all of us choose the same pathway."

"It's confusing."

"Why's that?"

"All that energy to make something wonderful, then to watch it disintegrate."

"Do you think that's part of his plan?"

"Naw. That would be a waste."

"Did God tell you that?"

"How would I even know if God told me something?"

"You'll know."

Down the valley the train whistled its approach. Seamoor turned and walked to catch his train.

"Next week we'll talk about the other part of God's plan."

The wind kicked up the leaves behind Seamoor as he blended into the scenery. Curiosity rubbed his eyes and squinted toward the station. Gone.

Who was this guy? How come his questions seemed to work their way so deeply into his thinking? It was clear that Seamoor was living a life with very little doubt, if any. Curiosity longed to live with this type of assurance.

Curiosity's Corner

Seamoor told me to keep the book. I thought he forgot it. Then I was thinking he had loaned it to me. Finally, he said it was mine. Seamoor is generous. He knows how to get inside my head, but he doesn't make me feel uncomfortable. We were talking about man being made in the image of God. If God made us in his image, I have to wonder just how much we actually act like him.

More from Seamoor

Genesis 1

Genesis 2:1-7

Hebrews 11:1

1 Thessalonians 2:13

Jeremiah 29:11

Week Three

Right and Wrong

"God always keeps His word."

Right and Wrong

Remembering that he had overlooked proper social etiquette the last time they met, Curiosity decided to be polite when he saw the older man.

"Good afternoon, Seamoor."

"Good afternoon to you as well. And a fine day it is."

"I fully agree. It's nice to see you."

Seamoor smiled.

"May I ask you more about creation?"

"I was hoping you would."

"Good. This is intriguing. How do we know God was there at the beginning?"

Seamoor waved his hand over the countryside.

"Who else do you think could have done all this?"

"Did it have to be God?"

"What does the book say?"

"The first few words are, *'In the beginning God created the heavens and the earth.'* Who wrote this?"

"Do you remember Moses?"

"Yeah, he led Israel out of slavery in Egypt."

"When Moses was leading Israel to the Promised Land, God had them stop at Mount Sinai and various places along the way. God called Moses to the top of the mountain. There he spoke to his prophet and began to tell him what to write. Moses was God's scribe for the first five books of the Bible."

"You're telling me God dictated this to Moses?"

"That's what I said."

"No wonder everyone talks about Moses and the Jews all the time."

"They are God's chosen people."

"Does that make them better than everyone else?"

"No, it means God uses them as an example for others."

"What kind of example?"

"God made promises to the Jews, whom he called Israel. When they did what he asked, God blessed them. When they didn't follow his instructions, they would have troubles. God always keeps his word."

"Always?"

"God created us to be like him. He teaches us to keep our promises."

"You are beginning to sound like my parents."

"That's right. God uses our parents to teach us his ways."

"So God tells Moses how he created us and everything else?"

"Yep."

"And Moses wrote it down."

"Yep."

"God wanted us to know about what he was doing?"

"Yep."

"That's flat-out amazing!"

"That's our God."

"So what happened to us?"

"We stopped studying his book."

"What for?"

"Because it tells us the difference between right and wrong."

"What's the matter with learning the difference between right and wrong?"

"There's nothing wrong with that, unless you want to make your own rules."

"Are you telling me we don't read this book because we want to be in charge?"

"I'm telling you people, even many of the people who read and study the Bible, still want to be in charge."

"So how can someone who believes this book not follow what it says?"

"It all gets back to what you mean by 'believe.'"

"I should say so."

"Tell me Curiosity, what do you believe?"

"That's a good question. Some of the things I used to believe don't match up with what I've been learning."

"That's one of the ways we grow."

"I'm even changing the way I think. Especially right now while we're talking."

"People change the way they think all the time."

"So how does God keep track of us? Does he know what we're thinking?"

"He knows it all. He knows what you are going to say before you say it."

"That scares me. What does he do if I'm going to do something wrong?"

"He doesn't stop you unless you are seriously messing with his plans."

"Wait a minute. You mean he lets us make mistakes?"

"Yes."

"Are we still responsible for our mistakes?"

"Yes."

"Oh boy. Am I ever in trouble."

"That's why he sent his Son."

"I don't understand. How would sending his Son help me with my mistakes?"

"This is the most wondrous thing God has ever done. God allows us to mess things up, then he shows us how he's going to fix it."

"Wow. You have such an amazing perspective on life."

"We need to look into the second section of the Bible. We've started looking at the Old Testament. It's time to look into the New Testament as well. Read the beginning of the book of John."

"Why are there two sections?"

"The second part was added when God sends his Son Jesus."

"Way cool."

Seamoor buttoned up his coat as he stood up. A woman with a baby carriage passed by. He glanced inside and waved at the child, then bid **"Good day"** to the mother. The woman looked at Curiosity.

"He's a nice gentleman."

Looking back at Curiosity, she nodded her head in accord. He returned his attention to Seamoor in time to see the back of his coat floating 'round the corner of the station platform.

Curiosity's Corner

Here's one for the book. God let's us make mistakes. While I know that we all make mistakes, the idea that God set this up so that he would send his Son Jesus to fix these mistakes is totally mind-blowing. Is that really God's plan? How can he fix our mistakes? That doesn't make sense. Seamoor asked me to read the New Testament book of John. I wonder if that will help me understand what's going on?

More from Seamoor

Psalm 33:4-12

Isaiah 42:5-9

Exodus 33:11

Isaiah 46:9-10

John 1:14

Week Four

Creation

"Yeshua came to take care of our mistakes."

Creation

Curiosity is almost breathless as he scurries over to meet Seamoor. He can't wait to start asking questions.

"Hi, Seamoor. It's great to see you."

"And I'm delighted to see you once again. What's on your mind?"

"I've never read anything like the book of John!"

"It sure opens your mind, doesn't it?"

"You've got that right. It's like lifting the fog. Everything looks different."

"That's what truth does."

"I was rethinking creation."

"Go on."

"In the first part of the book, God tells us how he began everything. But in the second part we discover Jesus was there with God right from the start."

Seamoor watched the expression of wonderment on Curiosity's face.

"Just where was God when he made everything?"

"We all wonder about that. Since God is Spirit, we can't limit him to space and time. He's everywhere. Always was. Always is. Always will be. When God introduced Himself to Moses, He said, 'I am that I am.'"

Curiosity shook his head in wonder. He looked up at a nearby robin joyfully chirping.

"My picture keeps getting bigger and bigger."

"That won't ever stop."

"But what did God and Jesus use to create the universe?"

"The Father, the Son, and the Holy Spirit—the Godhead—existed before time and brought the universe into being. Out of nothing known to the creation itself, God brought creation into existence."

"This is phenomenal."

"To say the least. You and I would not exist except for God."

"Nor would anything else exist."

"That's right."

"And he created it all for you and me?"

"Let's go back to the beginning. The book of Genesis tells us there were waters above the firmament, that is the heavens, and there were waters below. Then he separates the waters below to create the dry land from the waters above for the sky. So from these two waters, God creates the heavens and the earth."

"So that's how he did it?"

"That's what it says."

"And Jesus was with him while he did all of this."

"As well as the Holy Spirit."

"Wait. There are three of them?"

"For sure. If you look back at Genesis it tells us "...*the Spirit of God was hovering over the waters.*"

"So how does this work? You're telling me that all this was done by God, Jesus, and the Holy Spirit."

"That's why they call it the Holy Trinity."

Curiosity paused. Lots of pieces were falling into place. There was actually a written record of what God did. And he had help.

"Just how did God put all this together?"

"Only he has the answer to that. Think about the host of angels and whatever kind of assistance he needs to piece this together. And he did this in the heavens too, not just for us on earth."

"So the big bang theory is a much bigger bang than I can imagine."

"If that's what you want to call it. God tells us what he did, but we don't really know how he did it. And he hasn't stopped."

"Yeah, it's one thing to make all this, but how does he keep track of it all?"

"Just as you said, 'It keeps getting bigger and bigger.'"

"How does Jesus fit into this?"

"What did you learn in the first chapter of John?"

"It says nothing was made that was not made through him."

"What does that mean to you?"

"Jesus is involved with everything!"

"I like to use his Hebrew name, *Yeshua*. It means salvation."

"Salvation. So that's why everyone talks about get saved?"

"You've got it. When you get *Yeshua*, you get saved."

"Saved from what?"

"Saved from sin."

"I don't like that word 'sin.'"

"It's another word for 'mistake.' Remember when we talked about mistakes?"

"Unfortunately."

"*Yeshua* came to take care of our mistakes."

"Well I certainly like that."

"You're not going to find much of anything you don't like about *Yeshua*."

"I didn't think so."

"This book is God's gift to us. It shows us how he set things up for us. God reveals his plans, his love, his purposes for humanity."

"Why does God tell us his secrets?"

"Obviously we don't know most of what the Lord is doing. However, it's abundantly clear that he wants us to know that he is responsible for creation."

"I think God is watching us very closely."

The train whistle ended their conversation. Seamoor looked up at the robin and whistled in his direction. The bird flew over Curiosity's shoulder. He watched it settle on a nearby branch and whistle its reply. Looking back across the lawn, Curiosity noticed the elusive Seamoor had taken his leave.

Curiosity's Corner

Now we're talking about the Holy Trinity. Never really gave this much thought. It's like God can decide to be anything He wants. I tried to find out how creation works, but it seems as wise as Seamoor is, he's admitting that he doesn't have all the answers. Come to think of it, who would I believe to give me the answers to this? Seamoor did say that God tells us His secrets. What's that all about?

More from Seamoor

John 8:32

1 Corinthians 8:6

Psalm 104:30

John 1:29

Matthew 19:25-26

Week Five

Patience

"God will not allow anything to be overlooked."

Patience

Seamoor could see that Curiosity was agitated. After sitting down, he didn't speak for some time.

"What's on your mind?"

"Why do things take so long?"

"That depends on how you measure time."

"Don't you think that sometimes it takes too long for things to be accomplished?"

"Of course I do. Everybody thinks that way."

"I'm sure God has a different view on time than we do."

"Time is just our way of measuring infinity. We can't tell the beginning from the end. But God can. This is all part of his master plan."

"I suppose if I knew his master plan, then I would have a better understanding of time."

"When you have the entire universe to run, your understanding of time changes drastically."

"I can't imagine all the details that have to be coordinated."

"I don't think any of us will ever grasp the magnitude of God's plan."

"Nevertheless, it seems like some things never get done."

"Everything that is to be finished will be finished. God will not allow anything to be overlooked. Unlike us, he doesn't lose track of details."

"How is that possible?"

"That's one of the great mysteries of our God."

"I expect if we looked, we could find plenty of examples of things that don't get accomplished when they're supposed to. From the human standpoint, we see failure everywhere."

"In God's economy, failure has a unique and fulfilling purpose."

"That's the advantage he has in being God. He knows what's supposed to happen and he can make things happen when he wants them to."

"We are very limited in our perspective because we have difficulty measuring anything that lasts longer than our own lifetime. From an eternal point of view, a lifetime is just a breath of air."

"I feel very small when I think about God."

"That's actually a healthy response. Our biggest headaches occur when we start thinking too much of ourselves."

"It's hard for me not to push. I push myself to accomplish more and I push others when I think they could be doing more."

"What have the results been from pushing?"

"I'm not sure I'm getting any more accomplished."

"How about your relationship with your associates?"

"It's suffering. But we can't get time back, so I need to push."

"I would suggest that your timeline needs adjustment."

"I could use some clarification here."

"Patience is a virtue. The purpose of virtue is to teach us truth. If we lack patience, we don't live in truth."

"That's a heavy thought."

"Impatient people have difficulty seeing the truth for what it really is."

"How is that?"

"A lack of patience is a lack of faith. Patience is not so much about waiting as it is about expecting."

"Expecting what?"

"Expecting God to move."

"Wow. I didn't see that coming."

"A person of faith knows that God is in control. Knowing this makes waiting for something to happen much easier."

"That's really stepping out onto new ground for me. I get impatient because I don't know what's going to happen. Now you're telling me that you don't need to worry about things because God is in control."

"Well he is, you know."

"I'm not denying that, I'm just saying that we all have a part to play in this, and it takes people with some determination to get things done."

"I fully agree."

"So how am I going to get anything done without determination?"

"I thought the issue here was patience."

"It is."

"Patience and determination are not at odds with each other."

"It feels like they are."

"The distinction lies in who is taking the lead. In our struggle with patience, we leave God behind and become self-determined."

"That sounds like me."

"Let's consider reworking this equation by putting God first."

"What does that look like?"

"God waits for a very, very long time before passing judgment."

"That sounds wise."

"It's our absolute faith in God that keeps us calm. He will not fail. God is not swayed by personality. He discounts our errors and doesn't hold them against us. He is all loving, all forgiving."

"That's my God."

"He is color blind, gender neutral, indifferent to borders. He alone accepts our prayers and consecration. Though he dwells in peace, he is never passive."

"That's what I like to hear."

"He seeks those with a heart after him. He searches earth looking for pure hearts with a passion to find him, to serve him unashamedly and unapologetically. With those few faithful, he will build his Kingdom."

"I'm in."

Hooooot! The train was there and gone in an instant. Curiosity never knew what happened to Seamoor that afternoon.

Curiosity's Corner

Got into a really neat discussion about time. I'm getting a whole new download about patience. Seamoor has a way of getting me to reassess many of my assumptions. I've started to wonder about how God controls things. My confidence is rapidly increasing that everything is working under God's grand design. The best part is that I'm beginning to feel a genuine sense of peace I've never had before. But that's why I asked for Seamoor's help.

More from Seamoor

Psalm 145:8-9

Acts 10:34

Proverbs 16:9

Philippians 4:6-7

Revelation 22:13

Week Six

Our Peace

"And you're going to live to see it happen."

Our Peace

Seamoor was tossing a paper airplane into the wind. Curiosity stood by watching the elder enjoying himself.

"Looks like fun."

"Just the boy in me looking for expression."

"What does the boy want to say?"

"It's time to let our conversation fly."

"I can't wait. Let's get going."

"Where do you suppose peace comes from?"

"I'd guess it comes from God. That's who everybody asks for peace."

"I'd have to agree with you."

"Do you have a biblical passage to support this?"

"Ephesians chapter 2, verse 14: *'For He Himself is our peace.'*"

"It actually says that in the Bible?"

"Yes, it tells us that God's Son *Yeshua* is our peace. And it tells us how He makes peace."

"Don't stop now. Go on."

"It goes on to say that *Yeshua made both types of people into one*. Both types in this passage refer to both Jews and Gentiles."

"You're telling me that God's Son wants Jews and Gentiles to get along with each other?"

"You got it."

"That may take a miracle."

"And you're going to live to see it happen."

"I do hope so. How do we get there? Do you really think the Bible can teach us about peace?"

"Why not? As you said, it's the Word of God. Let's start in the same passage of Ephesians. Please read chapter 2, verses 14 through 18."

"OK. Here you go."

For **He Himself is our peace**, who has made both one, and has broken down the middle wall of separation, having abolished in His flesh the enmity, that is, the law of commandments contained in ordinances, so as to **create in Himself one new man from the two, thus making peace**, and that He might reconcile them both to God in one body through the cross, thereby putting to death the enmity. And **He came and preached peace** to you who were afar off and to those who were near. For through Him we both have access by one Spirit to the Father.

"**What do you think about that?**"

"There's a whole lot to absorb here."

"**If you're looking for world peace, it's a great place to start.**"

"All of a sudden the crucifixion takes on a much deeper meaning."

"**Most people don't stop long enough to take in God's plan. We're all too wrapped up in our own agendas to notice.**"

"This is God telling us how he's going to bring about world peace."

"**Not quite.**"

"What am I missing?"

"**You're talking about some future event.**"

"Exactly."

"**No. Not exactly.**"

"I thought you were showing me how God will bring us world peace."

"**He already has.**"

"He already has what?"

"**He already has brought about world peace.**"

"You could have fooled me."

"I don't want to fool you."

"Aren't you overlooking the headlines? Did you not notice the number of refugees? Haven't you heard about the genocides?"

"There is nothing new under the sun. The headlines today are just as terrible as they have always been."

"That's not a very positive view on life."

"I have a very positive view on life. It's seeing history repeat itself that makes me wonder if humanity will ever learn its lessons."

"That's tough. People can be very stubborn."

"Exactly the problem. God gives us the potential, but we shortchange him by not being willing to study history nor learn from our mistakes."

"So how can we have world peace if the world won't learn its lessons?"

"Good question. There are some who learn their lessons… but there are far too many who refuse to learn."

"What do we need to learn?"

"Humanity's plans for world peace don't work; can't work; never will work."

"Where's the hope if our plans don't or won't work?"

"Our hope is in God, the Maker of Heaven and earth. His plans never fail, never disappoint. They always work."

"You mean God's sovereign plans always prevail? You're telling me that God already knows what's going to happen."

"*Yeshua* already sealed the deal."

"The plans for world peace were set in place when *Yeshua* came here and died on that cross?"

"Precisely."

"How could we have missed that?"

"Humanity has been overlooking God's plans and his lovingkindness since the Garden of Eden. Each step we take toward God takes us closer to his peace."

"And each time we decide to go our own way, we move farther away."

"It's really that simple."

"I know it sounds easy, but you gotta believe."

"That's where you and I come in. God wants us to tell the world."

Hooooooot. Hooooooot. The men shook hands, turned, and parted company. Curiosity had finally received his answer about achieving world peace.

Curiosity's Corner

Not only am I rethinking time, I'm seeing that my concept of time won't work if I don't see why God sent *Yeshua* into the world. *Yeshua* reset our time clocks. Now I understand why we start our calendars with his birth. He is the only way we are going to get out of this mess. This changes everything! What amazes me is how I could have missed this. I thought I knew about finding world peace.

More from Seamoor

2 Thessalonians 3:16

1 Corinthians 14:33

Colossians 1:19-20

Isaiah 26:3

Isaiah 54:10

Week Seven

Leap of Faith

"You need spiritual eyes."

Leap of Faith

Curiosity started right in.

"There's something I don't understand."

"What's that?"

"Why did *Yeshua* need to die?"

"That's the question everyone who has ever lived wants to answer."

"Including me."

"He died for you and He died for me, too."

"That doesn't make sense. I never met him."

"With all due respect to you, my dear Curiosity, you're quite mistaken."

"Mistaken? Mistaken about what?"

"His death makes it possible for us to live."

"You've lost me."

"Well, we're all lost without *Yeshua*."

"I never knew him. He's never laid eyes on me."

"But He does know you."

"It's not possible for a man who died two thousand years ago to know me."

"Stay with me, Curiosity. His death has saved your life."

"How can that be? We've never had any contact."

"You're relying on your worldly vision. You need spiritual eyes."

"How do I do that?"

"You must be born again."

"I don't know how to do that. What good will that do anyway?"

"It's a leap of faith."

"A leap from where? And where am I supposed to land?"

"It's a leap from darkness into light."

"What is this darkness?"

"Darkness is a place without vision. God gives us vision so we can see the places where we need him in our lives."

"I don't know about other people, but I see way too many places in my life where I need help. It's impossible."

"With people it's not possible, but with God, all things *are* possible."

"This faith thing is really a test."

"It can be for many. It requires letting go of your blindness."

"Letting go of blindness? I see just fine."

"I mean letting go of your past beliefs. They won't help you get to where you need to go. In fact, they can prevent you from getting close to God."

"How can you tell me where I need to go?"

"I once stood where you're standing."

"How could you know where I stand?"

"I don't claim to know the position where you stand. I know the condition that you are in."

"What condition is that?"

"It's the same condition we all have when we are born the first time. We're all imperfect in need of a savior. That's why I repeated what *Yeshua* said, 'You must be born again.' It's a leap from darkness into light."

"That sounds like a very negative view on life. How can God be a just God if he sets it up for everyone who is born to be born with problems."

"From the very beginning God demonstrates his great care for us by taking us out of darkness into the light of his love. He did it with creation and he continues to do it every day with salvation.

"How does that work?"

"God's salvation is his way of displaying his love for us. He demonstrates his mercy by forgiving us. He demonstrates his grace by separating us from our sin. He demonstrates his lovingkindness by allowing his own Son, the most precious person in all the universe, to give up his life that we might conquer death and live for eternity."

"That's such an amazing plan. How do we know that it's true?"

"The best answer is the testimony of changed lives. Once people are born again, newfound values lift them and carry them through life's trials and tribulations. God's love makes us different."

"Now I know why they call the gospel the good news."

"That's why those of us who have taken the leap have a calling on our lives. Once a person receives God's gift of eternal life, nothing else will ever compare to that magnificent blessing."

"I need to do some soul searching."

"May I suggest you don't go there alone? Ask *Yeshua* to help you with this."

"I'll take all the help I can get."

"Good. You are not alone on your journey."

"Where do you suggest I start?"

"When the first disciples needed help, they asked *Yeshua* how to pray."

"What did *Yeshua* say to them?"

"He taught them the Lord's Prayer. You know it. Let's say this together."

"Our Father in heaven, hallowed be your name. Your kingdom come. Your will be done on earth as it is in heaven. Give us this day our daily bread. And forgive us our debts, as we forgive our debtors. And do not lead us into temptation, but deliver us from the evil one. For Yours is the kingdom and the power and the glory forever. Amen."

That day Curiosity never heard the train come, nor did he notice Seamoor's departure. When he opened his eyes, everything was a picture of tranquility.

Curiosity's Corner

Something remarkable happened today. I prayed the Lord's Prayer with Seamoor and everything shifted. I mean every little thing. I could feel God. I experienced real peace. I knew my life was never going to be the same. Things that were abstract are falling into place. One day I'm looking for peace, and then I find it. I decided to follow *Yeshua*. He is the answer. I never thought I'd hear myself say this, "Praise God! Hallelujah!"

More from Seamoor

Philippians 1:21

John 3:3-5

1 Peter 2:9-10

Ephesians 2:1-10

John 3:16-17

God wants to be real with us

Rending

Science
Love
Connecting the Dots
Walk in Unity
Outside Thinking
Family
Purple Ticket

Week Eight

Science

"*Science is never satisfied with today's answers.*"

Science

Today Curiosity is already seated awaiting the elder. The younger playfully dusts off the bench.

"Good day to you, kind sir."

"And to you."

"Ready to go?"

"Most assuredly. Tell me, how can you be sure God loves us?"

"He says so in his book."

"This book is so old."

"We spoke of that before. Is this a compliment or a criticism?"

"I suppose it's both."

"Let's delve into this. If we regard the book's message to be timeless and its source all-knowing, it's safe to say it's a compliment.

"Agreed."

"If it lacks relevance because it's out of touch with reality, then it's a criticism."

"Agreed."

"Shall we approach this by affirming the complimentary approach or by disproving its lack of relevancy?"

"I'd like to hear both perspectives."

"I believe this is the wisest choice. You'll see these are connected."

"How can you claim that decisions made thousands of years ago hold weight in a world bearing little resemblance to that era?"

"In the realm of the spirit, there are no time restrictions. So the types of spirits we encounter today are the same as those that existed long ago."

"When you say, 'types of spirits,' I'm not sure what you mean. How am I to recognize a spirit?"

"One way of recognizing spirits is through emotions. If I speak of the spirit of love or jealousy, do you understand?"

"Sure."

"Would these same spirits be any different now than when this book was written?"

"No."

"Therefore, advice about fixing broken relationships is not limited by whatever era we live in."

"Granted, the Bible teaches valuable things. But how can you compare a world lacking electricity and running water to our culture today?"

"First, let's remember, far too many on the face of the earth today lack such advantages. Your comparison is limited to the fortunate ones who live in economically prosperous locations."

"Science has advanced to heights never dreamed of by the early church."

"Science is a form of investigation. Science hasn't changed its role since the days of Pharaoh's sorcerers. Science is never satisfied with today's answers. It always seeks further proof."

"Is that bad?"

"Of course not. However, you seek *relevance*. There is a relevance to the Bible and there is a relevance to science. They're not the same."

"What's the difference?"

"Seeking further proof is good. It increases our knowledge of both God and science. Proof in God requires genuine faith that He exists. God expects us to find him in his creation, in his love, and in his goodness."

"How can you prove these things?"

"The Bible proclaims, *'Without faith it is impossible to please God.'*"

"Are you saying there's no concrete proof of God?"

"**I'm saying the earth, emotions, and even life itself are proof of God.**"

"Where does that leave science?"

"**Science begins with the known to seek the unknown. God begins with the unknown to create the known. Science is limited if it lacks faith in God. Proof in God is unlimited because all it needs is faith.**"

"Meaning that science discourages faith?"

"**I'm referring to faith in God. When science encourages faith in physical evidence, it does so with the expectation its followers will put their faith in science. But science built without faith in God will always be limited. Such science demands a different type of faith.**"

"So faith in science must be limited to known data."

"**Do you see the dilemma scientists have created for themselves? Faith cannot be limited. Faith in science falls far short of faith in God.**"

"But I'm saying science, just like the Bible, can teach me some valuable things."

"**I'm not saying science is without value. I'm cautioning us to not put our faith into something that reduces flexible thinking.**"

"So is there something wrong with science?"

"**Quite the contrary. Science is wonderful. God wants us to increase in knowledge. But faith in science diminishes our faith to the level of belief on what is known or provable. This is not real faith. You can't walk on water by using proof. Scientific proof tells you that you will sink.**"

"What is real faith?"

"**Real faith is like real love. You can't prove it in the physical world, but you know it's there.**"

"Like trying to prove a miracle."

"**Aha. Can you prove a miracle without faith?**"

"You can't."

"**Our relationship with God starts with faith. The Bible only proves God exists if you have the faith to believe what it says. The more you read the Bible, the more your faith will grow.**"

Curiosity didn't notice the whistle. Starting to ask the next question, he suddenly realized Seamoor had disappeared.

Curiosity's Corner

I always wondered how science fits into the big picture. I didn't realize that I didn't grasp what the big picture is. Without God, there is no big picture. Science does its best to come up with impressive answers and statistics. But there's a realm of faith that science doesn't account for. God has answers to questions science hasn't even asked. How ironic that science's way of measuring the unknown things is restricted. God has no limits.

More from Seamoor

Psalm 147:5

Psalm 86:15

Proverbs 30:4

Hosea 14:9

James 1:6

Week Nine

Love

"How's that for real power?"

Love

Seamoor was humming as Curiosity sat next to him.

"How are you doing?"

"Just fine. How about you?"

"I'm quite well. Thanks for asking."

"You know we never really got around to talking about love."

"I noticed that too."

"Why do you suppose that was?"

"There are many issues that distract us from the main thing."

"And the main thing is love."

"There you go."

"We were talking about faith."

"That's where we need to start. Faith in a loving God."

"God doesn't have much meaning without faith."

"We can talk about faith, but that's not the same as having it."

"So where does love come in?"

"Love is what makes this all possible. Without love our world would never have come into existence. God did not come to create a world of darkness. What was the first thing God said?"

"Let there be light."

"Right you are! What do you think light is?"

"The opposite of darkness."

"Not quite."

"Huh?"

"Darkness is the absence of light."

"Isn't that what I said?"

"You said it was the opposite. I'm saying it is the absence."

"Clue me in on this. What's the difference?"

"To say something is the opposite is to say it holds equal value in the opposing direction. This means darkness would have as much power as light. But darkness is the *absence* of light. Darkness is void. It is emptiness. Without light, darkness has no meaning or purpose."

"I seem to remember reading something like that."

"I see you brought your Bible. Turn to the first chapter of John. The first few verses deal with this. Why not start with verse 5?"

"And the light shines in the darkness, and the darkness did not comprehend it."

"You can see that light is stronger than darkness."

"I got it."

"In the same way, faith is stronger than doubt."

"Yeah, we're saying doubt is the absence of faith, not the opposite."

"You picked right up on that. Now we're ready to talk about love."

"Wait. Don't tell me. Love overpowers fear. I've always heard that, but I didn't know how it worked."

"The Bible says, 'Perfect love casts out fear.' How's that for real power?"

"Awesome."

"We are learning how to apply biblical principles to life. That's why we need God's Word to guide our steps."

Seamoor holds up the Bible. Curiosity's gaze follows its motion as it crosses in front of the sun. He squints at the light.

"The book of John says, *'In Him* [meaning *Yeshua*] *was life, and the life was the light of men.'"*

"When God says. *'Let there be light,'* He was also referring to the light of His Son *Yeshua.*"

"Well said. When God sends *Yeshua* to be that light, the reason is *'God so loved the world that He gave His one and only Son.'"*

"That means the Bible can teach me about love."

"I'll do you one better. The Bible is God's handbook on love. Read on a bit and you'll see there's more. There's a connection between love and light and *Yeshua.*"

"I'm not surprised. Love isn't just some abstract idea or an emotion. It's based on God's plan for us. And this book lays it all out."

"Let's follow this pathway. God creates the universe out of His love for us. He begins the process by bringing light and life to earth. That life moves from the cradle of creation to cover the earth with our Lord's great love."

"This Bible is a whole lot more than just a book."

"It's God's book. It's His Word. Our Father sent His Son as His Word in human form. Yeshua is the incarnate, infallible, incontestable Word of God. Almighty God gives us His written Word to be His blueprint for righteous living. He then sends *Yeshua* to enter His creation as a man to confirm every word recorded in His book is true."

"I've never heard of anything so overwhelming in all my life."

"To accept the word of the Old Testament is to accept Jesus. *Yeshua* personifies God's written testament. He is these God-inspired words made flesh."

"How did you figure out all this stuff?"

"I didn't have to figure at all. It's in His book. I love to share the story of God's creation and the sending of *Yeshua*."

"Not half as much as I enjoy hearing it. I think I'd better do some more reading."

The whistle blast of the soon-arriving train startled Curiosity. He waved good-bye and was back into the book of John. Seamoor grinned as he stepped toward the tracks. This day Curiosity was too preoccupied to attempt to discern the prophet's disappearance.

Curiosity's Corner

Somehow we all know that love is the glue that holds this whole thing together. But what I didn't get until today is that *Yeshua* is love personified. I mean, I get that we love people, but I never expected to discover that God actually came in the form of a human being to save us. We're all running in circles trying to figure out how to ignite the light of peace. It already shines as *Yeshua*.

More from Seamoor

Ephesians 3:16-19

John 15:13

1 John 4:19

Hebrews 4:12

Galatians 2:20

Week Ten

Connecting the Dots

"The stepping stones to peace."

Connecting the Dots

Curiosity was full of vim and vigor as he approached Seamoor. His mentor could see the look of enthusiasm on the pupil's face.

"Hello. How are you this beautiful day?"

"I'm so excited by what I'm reading. I don't know where to begin."

"Did you learn anything new?

"This might sound funny, but I am beginning to see how God sees things."

"Good for you. It's time to connect some dots."

"Sounds like fun. Which dots?"

"Faith, hope, and love."

"Sounds like the Holy Trinity."

"That's not a bad analogy."

"Aha. How are they connected?"

"We find these three—faith, hope, and love—mentioned together at the end of First Corinthians chapter 13. This is the famous passage about love. God tells us that no matter what we think, do, or accomplish, if we don't have love it doesn't count for anything."

"That sounds like the kind of God I want to honor."

"These three form the bedrock of God's plans for us. He did more than create this world, God also expects us to honor his pathway to unity. These three are the stepping stones to peace."

"OK. Help me to get my mind around this. Let's start with faith."

"Faith is the substance of things hoped for, the evidence of realities not seen."

"That must be from the Bible. Where is it?"

"The book of Hebrews, chapter 11, verse 1. This is the beginning of 'Faith's Hall of Fame.' Here we discover the way God blesses those who believe."

"Then this goes back to deciding where we put our faith."

"Well put. We all have faith in something. We exercise our highest calling when we put our faith in God."

"In God We Trust."

"It's no accident we put that phrase on our money. We need to be constantly reminded we trust in God, not material wealth."

"Sort of ironic that the thing we strive for points us back to the One who makes all this possible. Money—the ultimate material possession—says there's something, or should I say someone, where we need to put our faith."

"The Bible teaches that the love of money is a root of all evil."

"Even our money directs us where to put our trust. I love it."

"This also tells us there is such a thing as evil and our choices have consequences. God allows us to make choices, then He causes us to experience the results of these choices."

"So what's the result of exercising our faith in God?"

"In a word, we discover love—faith allows us to experience God's love. From the time a baby first cries for attention and receives a mother's hug, up to the moment we take our last breath, we are surrounded by the atmosphere of God's love."

"And the reason that we don't see this is?"

"Because the thing we need is invisible without faith. Faith gives substance and meaning to the invisible."

"Wow. That's quite a reach. Yet it makes sense."

"The power behind our faith is our willingness and courage to believe. Our faith leads to hope."

"Wonderful. Where does hope come in?"

"Hope is faith magnified. Faith comes as the result of a decision to believe. Hope comes when one's belief is focused on God. There is nothing more frustrating and painful than false hope; just as there is nothing more heartening and fulfilling than having one's hope fulfilled."

"You can say that again. It's tough when I can't get something I really want."

"That's why children, and even some grown ups, throw temper tantrums. Sometimes, if we make a big enough stink, we get what we think we really want."

"But that's not going to help the person grow."

"Right you are! Because that's not healthy growth based on faith, it's manipulation. It leads us *away* from God, not *toward* him."

"For sure. That kind of behavior doesn't lead us to God."

"These people prefer to use human weakness instead of divine faith."

"Such individuals play on human emotions."

"So true. Human emotions are remarkably powerful. We should not underestimate them. But faith and hope are stronger than emotions."

"Emotions are compelling. They drive us and impact our lives."

"Emotions determine the depth of imprint into our memories."

"If faith and hope are stronger than emotions, then we are really heading for high ground. Where does that leave love?"

The forlorn signal drifted down the tracks to the glen where the two conversed.

"Love will meet us next week."

Seamoor rose and turned to go. Curiosity couldn't take his eyes off him. Seamoor strode down the path and through a small grove of trees and vanished.

Curiosity's Corner

There is a connection between faith, hope, and love. I hear people read about this at their weddings, but I haven't given these things the thought they deserve. I realize the substance of faith is more real than our material world. And hope doesn't exist without the seed of faith. Can't wait to learn more about love. I've got to study Ephesians. Love is the greatest expression of God. I wish more people knew God loved them.

More from Seamoor

1 John 4:7

1 Peter 4:8

Galatians 5:16-17

Proverbs 24:14

Romans 5:1-5

Week Eleven

Walk in Unity

"Shines like light in a dark place."

Walk in Unity

Curiosity spent the previous evening reading passages in the book of Ephesians. He remembered Seamoor's words about the "One New Man." He was fascinated by what he saw.

"Hello, Seamoor. Guess what I've been doing?"

"Why do I think you're going to tell me you've been in the Word of God?"

"Right you are."

"Did you see anything that interested you?"

"You know I did. I started to learn about unity."

"Marvelous."

"God's plans for peace are much bigger than I expected."

"Really?"

"Aww, come on now. You know what it says."

Curiosity playfully nudged his mentor. Seamoor finally cracked a smile.

"So you're beginning to see the light."

"I think I may need to wear sunglasses just to read this book."

"Aha. So what's important about unity?"

"God wants everyone to do this together. I've always heard people talk about getting things 'together,' but they don't know the depth of what they are saying. More than that, it appears God had planned this right from the start!"

"I must agree with you."

"How can God know how things will end up? How does anyone know the future before it happens? That's crazy."

"So you think God is crazy?"

"I don't know what God is, but knowing the future is beyond reason. There are too many variables. No one can know it all."

"So even the most reasonable people can't outthink God."

"No one is ever going to outthink God."

"Don't tell those scientists who deny him, because he defies reason."

"They might be offended by such a remark."

"So what's God's plan for unity?"

"Shouldn't I be asking you that question?"

"Your Bible uses the same words that mine does. Isn't it clear?"

"I studied this last night. It's in Ephesians in the beginning of chapter 4. The subtitle says, 'Walk in Unity.'"

"Let's hear it."

Curiosity cleared his throat. He held up the Bible and spoke with a notable reverence. You could hear that he was genuinely impressed with its significance.

I, therefore, the prisoner of the Lord, beseech you to walk worthy of the calling with which you were called, with all lowliness and gentleness, with longsuffering, bearing with one another in love, endeavoring **to keep the unity of the Spirit in the bond of peace.** *There is one body and one Spirit, just as you were called in one hope of your calling; one Lord, one faith, one baptism; one God and Father of all, who is above all, and through all, and in you all.*

"You read that well. What do you make of it?"

"Well, we're told that unity is a function of the Spirit. We've got this high call to do what God wants us to do. That requires us to be humble so we can show his love to each other. By doing this we are unified. God asks us to seek this unity by his Spirit and to be connected to each other as examples of peace.

"Magnificently stated. See, you understand what it says."

"I'm only beginning to understand. There's more. He tells us about the meaning of "one." It covers the whole territory of walking out our faith. It's a beautiful picture of how God wants us to be united as one."

"Sounds good to me."

"Me too. The last sentence really informs me. God is above, through, and in all creation, including you, me, and everyone else. It's time to pitch out all our man-made counterfeit faiths. This one shines."

"Shines like light in a dark place."

"Then it gets difficult."

"Go on."

"We are asked to walk with lowliness, gentleness, long suffering, and bearing with each other."

"What's wrong with that?"

"It sounds like we are going to get thrashed. Who wants that?"

"How would you express love?"

"I don't know. But who wants to get beat up and belittled?"

"Sounds like *Yeshua*. Why do you think he did that?"

"I don't know."

"Because he loves you."

"Me? Jesus loves me? How do you know that?"

"The Word of God says, 'We love Him because He first loved us.' There are numerous scriptures about God's love for us. We're His children."

"I'd enjoy hearing one."

First John 4:10-11 says, *"This is love—not that we loved God, but that He loved us and sent His Son as an atonement for our sins. Loved ones, if God so loved us, we also ought to love one another."*

"What beautiful words. Why do I know that the train is about to arrive?"

"I'll see you next week."

Sure enough, the rushing sound of the train comes whistling through the trees. And Seamoor is gone with the wind.

Curiosity's Corner

The beauty of reading scripture is that it explains things that no other book knows how. I now see that unity is a model of God's love. We show people his love when we get connected. No connection—no love. I can see that love will never be the same for me. I've got to learn how to be more attentive and compassionate. Funny how I see my role is making a difference instead of criticizing others.

More from Seamoor

Ephesians 1:18

Mark 3:25

1 Corinthians 1:10

1 Corinthians 6:17

John 17:21

Week Twelve

Outside Thinking

" It's the internal desires that drive us."

Outside Thinking

Curiosity was greatly relieved to see Seamoor at his regular spot on the park bench.

"Good morning, Seamoor. I've had a tough week."

"Good morning."

"Aren't you going to ask me why it was tough?"

"Aren't you going to tell me?"

"Of course. I kept running into conflicts with my friends and family. I wanted to tell them about *Yeshua*. Some were interested, but my parents had no desire to know. My mom rolled her eyes up to the ceiling."

"Have you had conversations like this before with your family?"

"We've had disagreements. Everybody does. But I don't know that I've ever felt so disrespected for something that I feel is this important."

"Did you argue?"

"Yeah."

"Did it do you any good?"

"I think it made things worse."

"So what happens next?"

"I don't know. I've given it lots of thought."

"That's good."

"Being humble sounds easy, but it's really hard. I want people to listen to me, but the harder I push the more they resist. I don't know that I have the patience to walk this thing out."

"Humility and patience are learned skills. They don't just happen."

"Well it looks like I have a lot to learn. Is this going to take long?"

"You already know the answer to that question. We never stop learning. It takes a lifetime. Some lessons are tougher than others. And some lessons we just don't want to learn."

"Why is that?"

"Because we hold on to stuff that we don't need. Letting go of our character flaws requires some real hard work."

"I don't know how I'm going to accomplish this."

"I know how you feel. The task seems daunting. But the bigger the problem, the more opportunity there is for God to show his power. There isn't anything he can't fix."

"OK. Now we're getting into an area that puzzles me. If God can fix anything, and he's so great, why doesn't he just fix it? Things are a mess on this planet. We could sure use some serious assistance."

"Just what do you think he ought to do?"

"I think he ought to make things easier for us."

"So in light of our conversations, would making things easier unify us?"

"I'd hope so. If people got more food and things didn't cost so much, we'd get along better."

"Is that so?"

"You sound skeptical."

"I am questioning the outcome of your thinking."

"Where's the challenge?"

"Can you show me a place where there is plenty to eat and things cost less where there is more unity?"

"Not off hand."

"Do you think you're the first person who wants things easier?"

"I think everybody wants things easier."

"That's probably true. Does making things easier make for more peace?"

"If everybody got what they needed we would start running out of things to fight about."

"I hear your approach, but this is what I call 'outside thinking.'"

"Outside of what?"

"We have this idea that meeting our *external* needs will also satisfy our *internal* needs. We think that getting enough to eat leads to peace."

"Well it's a good place to start."

"That may be, but things don't end there. In the end, it's the internal desires that drive us. We want affirmation. We want significance. We want our lives to count for something. Don't you?"

"Absolutely."

"If we don't have these passions met, all the food and all the money in the world won't be enough. I'm not denying the necessity of sustenance and personal needs. Lasting harmony requires functional relationships. This is the food, the fuel, that satisfies the soul. This is what's on the inside."

"How does this affect our relationship with God?"

"The way we treat each other speaks of how we treat God. We cannot claim we care about God if we aren't concerned with the needs of others, including food and shelter."

"For sure."

"Life is precious and must be nurtured, but life is more than physical needs. Life is relational. Life is personal. Our emotional and psychological needs outweigh our physical needs."

"How does God prioritize all of this?"

"He asks us to put him first. That's what he did with us. Our spiritual needs override all of the others. If we start with our spiritual health, all the other needs we have will improve immediately."

The inevitable whistle brought the conversation to a close.

"Thanks, Seamoor."

"Thank you, Curiosity. You're growing swiftly."

Today Curiosity didn't try to watch Seamoor leave. He closed his eyes and listened. There was a quiet swish behind him as if the air had suddenly been released from a sealed container. Then all was quiet.

Curiosity's Corner

I was so excited to tell everyone about *Yeshua*. Then it all blew up in my face. It's like the ones I care about the most don't realize how important this is to me. I thought they'd be jumping for joy. Instead they're jumping down my throat. Why isn't this working? Everything I'm learning is so right. Where did I get off track? Is this what it's like to follow *Yeshua?* So glad Seamoor has my back.

More from Seamoor

Psalm 25:9

Titus 2:7-8

Romans 12:2

Romans 14:19

Matthew 6:33

Week Thirteen

Family

"Unity satisfies the law of attraction."

Family

Seamoor was dozing when Curiosity arrived. He sat down quietly. A few moments later the elder awoke.

"Have you been here long?"

"Just a couple of months."

"Oh good. I was afraid it was a long time."

Both men snickered with glee.

"Tell me please, where do we learn about unity?"

"In the family."

"That's a good answer."

"The best example I can think of is the love parents have for their own children. We see this strong instinct reflected in nature."

"Like a mama bear protects her cubs."

"You've got it. The family is the safest place on earth: a father and mother to provide and nurture, brothers and sisters to share. It's a place to gather, a place to grow."

"A place of safety and refuge."

"If people start without family, they spend their lives looking for significance. That's how strong this is. It's our first identity."

"Our first identity?"

"Yes. That's the identity we're born with. We don't get a new identity until we are born again."

"OK. I see. We are first born into our earthly family, then the second time we are born again into a kingdom family."

"You're right on target. But it's even better than that. Your kingdom family lasts for eternity. Imagine that!"

"*Yeshua's* death actually opened up a place in God's family for us to join him."

"I never heard it put that way. That's a beautiful thought."

"Wow. Thanks."

"The ultimate example of love happens when God gives his very own Son."

"It boggles my mind whenever I think of it."

"*Yeshua* asked God that we would be one. His last prayer was for unity. Our Father knows how much unity means. Psalm 133 teaches us that God commands a blessing when we are unified, when we are a family."

"You were telling me about unity and peace. How does this work?"

"Unity is the pathway to peace. To find peace, we first need unity. World peace, the kind of peace you're talking about, needs fellowship."

"OK."

"Unity satisfies the law of attraction. We all need companionship. Our needs differ with every individual, but every individual has needs."

"Can you give me an example?"

"Of course, there are the obvious physical needs of food and shelter. But food and shelter aren't enough. Adam and Eve had that. They even had fellowship with God. But there was a hunger for more. They looked beyond what God had supplied."

"And what would that be?"

"Lust. Lust for more than what they had received from God Almighty. The serpent in the Garden of Eden questioned

God's authority. He convinced Adam and Eve that following their Creator wasn't enough."

"That sounds like a formula for disaster. Why do you say, 'Lust'?"

"People who aren't satisfied with God want to be their own gods. They lust for power, lust for significance, lust for dominance, lust for control."

"Where does lust come from?"

"Lust is a manifestation of pride. Our enemy traps us by making us believe we will get more by going our own way. So the devil plays on our pride. He convinces us that we are entitled to whatever we want."

"That's living without restraints. How does that differ from freedom?"

"Freedom implies something harmful has been removed. The Garden was secure except for that serpent. It was there that humanity was tempted and fell. Left to our own devices we fail miserably."

"I like having things my own way."

"We all do. Seeking independence is an important part of growth, but that's not to be confused with submitting to godly authority. If we fail to serve God, pride will fill the void. Pride is humankind's response to the desire for our own significance."

"So when people seek to control others, they yield to pride."

"Pride insists on superiority. There is a haughty, arrogant spirit behind pride. When this spirit yields to lust, it becomes perverted."

"I don't think we realize how much trouble we're in without God. I can see why people who are isolated are easy pickings for the enemy of our souls. Is there a connection between love and lust?"

"Lust is love out of control. Lust is love turned inside out. Lust makes loving myself more important than loving others.

Lust twists the purity of love into perversion. Sometimes we mislabel it as passion. It isn't until we see the damage our own agenda inflicts that we discover how badly we need God. *Yeshua* **says, '*Without me, you can do nothing.*'"**

On that note, the train came 'round the bend. Steam from its engines swept across the parkway, obscuring Seamoor's exit, swallowing him in the smoke.

Curiosity's Corner

It is shocking for me to discover how vulnerable I am, as well as the rest of the world, to my own weaknesses. I haven't given enough thought to my need for love—for the right kind of love. Everyone is trying so hard to be accepted, yet we have overlooked the fact that God shows his acceptance by putting us together with the right people. The One who really loves is the One who won't judge.

More from Seamoor

2 Corinthians 6:18

Galatians 4:7

Jude 16-19

2 Peter 1:3-4

John 13:35

Week Fourteen

Purple Ticket

"Your ticket was paid for."

Purple Ticket

Curiosity sat on the park bench looking at his watch. He turned up his collar against the wind. Seamoor was nowhere to be found. It was past their usual rendezvous time. He was a little nervous something might have happened to his friend.

"It's a beautiful day!"

"There you are. I thought something was wrong."

"Nothing wrong. I wondered if you wanted to ride the train today."

"Sure. I've often wondered where you go when you leave."

"Oh, I'm always on call."

"Huh?"

The familiar whistle caught their attention.

"Hurry up or we'll miss her."

"I'm on my way."

Instantly the two of them were boarding a mysterious train. It had a glass floor with rows of wooden benches. No walls, no ceiling. All the benches were empty.

"Take a seat."

Both settled on the nearest bench. As they left the station, there was no sound of an engine or the familiar clickety-clack of wheels on rails. They were traveling rapidly, yet there was only a gentle breeze. Strange. Curiosity was elated. Seamoor smiled as he observed the young apprentice.

"What on earth is this?"

"Who said we were on earth?"

Curiosity chuckled.

"So where are we?"

"I thought you wanted to see what's happening on the inside."

"I'm ready."

"Good."

The train was passing through objects. Right through mountains that didn't seem to exist in the physical. Down into rivers, underwater without getting wet. Everything was luminous. No bumps. No sense of gravity.

When his eyes returned to the train, all the benches were filled. All kinds of people. All types of clothes. All different ages. Everyone was laughing and pretty much oblivious to the scenery. Many held hands. All looked intently into the eyes of the one each accompanied.

"I like this place."

"I was sure you would. What do you like the most?"

"It's so peaceful and beautiful. I've never felt such serenity."

"This is the inside."

"How did we get here?"

"You decided to follow."

"Follow? Follow whom?"

"*Yeshua*."

"Hold on. I didn't tell anyone."

"You prayed it last night."

"I was going to tell you today."

"Word got out the moment you decided."

"There are no secrets in this place."

"There's no need for secrets here."

"Help me understand. I prayed and told *Yeshua* I wanted to follow him."

"That's right."

"It's that easy?"

"Well, yes and no. For some people it's very easy. For others, they have a hard time getting here. Many never make the choice."

"They don't know what they're missing."
"No, they don't."
"What's it cost to take the train?"
"Nothing for you."
"What does that mean?"
"Your ticket was paid for."
"Do I owe you anything?"
"My ticket was paid for too."
"Who paid for our tickets?"
"I think you know who."

Seamoor handed him a purple ticket stub. Curiosity stuffed it into his pocket.

"This is too good to be true."
"Truth is far better than people believe."
"Does anybody know about this place?"
"Yeah, lots of people know about this place."
"I hope not too many. If word ever got out it would be overrun."
"Word has gone out."
"Then why aren't there more people?"
"Because you have to believe."
"Is that how I got here?"
"Yes."
"Thank God."
"Yes. Thank God."

Curiosity had never felt such tranquility. He closed his eyes and drew in his breath. Everything smelled forest fresh. The sounds were crisp and distinct. Waves of joy passed through his body. He had never felt so alive, so aware. Opening his eyes once more, the colors of nearby fields sparkled with purity and brilliance. He blinked and the radiance of light permeated his very being.

Seamoor handed Curiosity a wooden stick with what appeared to be a drop of nectar on it. He motioned for me to taste it. When it touched my tongue, my mouth exploded with delight. Sweetness I had never imagined overwhelmed my senses. Yet there was a calm and quietness that kept everything in perfect balance.

Curiosity didn't want to move. He sat in a state of pure contentment. There were no questions in his mind. His quest for the unknown had been thoroughly satisfied. Oh that all of humanity would discover what God has done.

A whistle distracted Curiosity. He sat up. He was on the park bench. No one was next to him. No sign of Seamoor. He looked at his watch. Less than a minute had gone by. Was all of this a dream? Leaning forward, he gathered his jacket tighter. He noticed something in his pocket. He pulled it out. A purple railway ticket. Only now the ticket had a hole punched through it.

Curiosity's Corner

Today I visited Heaven. Seamoor was late. He asked me to ride the train with him. I got on board and the next thing I knew we were traveling through another dimension. Seamoor knew I had accepted *Yeshua* to be my Lord and Savior. There's no longer any question in my mind about miracles. I just had one. I suppose it's no wonder that no one else was there to witness. It's just between me and *Yeshua*.

More from Seamoor

Mark 10:15

Matthew 6:10

1 John 2:2

Ecclesiastes 3:11

Revelation 21:1-27

God wants to be with us always

Never-Ending

Perfection
Changing Direction
Potential
Walls
Joy
One New Man
Godly Government

Week Fifteen

Perfection

"Imperfect people do His perfect work."

Perfection

Curiosity was deep in thought when he arrived at the park bench.

"Good day to you, young man."

"And a fine day it is. Very peaceful."

"So it is…but I expect it will get cloudy."

"We could use some rain. So what does God expect from us?"

"Got wants us to be perfect. To be perfect in his sight."

"You've got to be kidding. There's no way that we could ever be perfect."

"That depends on your definition of 'perfect.'"

"I think I'm about to learn something new."

"Ha ha. God always has something new for us. Just as some would object to the coming rain, nothing will grow without water. God uses both the sun and the rain. That doesn't mean that wet weather is bad."

"Of course. And we all like sunny weather, but rain is necessary. Can we say the same of sin? Is it necessary?"

"Sin is the way God leads us to himself. When we realize that we can't make it without God to correct our faulty behavior, we discover only God is good enough to make things right."

"I certainly never looked at things that way."

"It is in our imperfection that we see our need for God."

"So how are we going to be perfect when the Word of God says that we sin?"

"That's a real good question. The Word of God says all have sinned and fallen short of the glory of God."

"Well, doesn't that prove that we can't be perfect?"

"God has ways of forgiving us of our sins."

"That would have to be God, because I don't get it. I thought this whole gift of salvation is somehow set up around us needing forgiveness for our sins."

"It's true that we need forgiveness for our sins. The Lord has ways of dealing with sin that surpass our own understanding. God wants us to look to him for our answers."

"How does looking to him make us perfect?"

"Once we turn to God with genuine repentance, he can perfect us."

"Help me with what you mean by repentance."

"It simply means turning away from what you were doing wrong. And having recognized your sin, you don't go back and do it again."

"That makes sense. Let me review this. First comes sin. Next, we need to recognize that we all suffer from sin. Then comes our repentance."

"That's right."

"OK. Now take me back to perfection."

"We start out being made in the very image of God. Yet we are born as helpless infants without the ability to walk, speak, or control our bodily functions."

"I remember when my little brother was born. We had to do everything for him. But he sure knew how to cry."

"That's how babies communicate. Adults cry out to God as well."

"I guess we need help, just like our own children."

"God gives us the right to become his children. We are adopted into his family. When we accept *Yeshua*, the perfection begins."

"So perfection needs a starting place. That's deep. Isn't being made in God's image enough?"

"It's not just our DNA. God perfects us through relationship. It's more than a state of being. We grow in our relationship with God, just as we grow in our relationships with each other."

"OK, but just because someone has accepted *Yeshua* doesn't mean the person stops doing things wrong. I know a lot of people who believe in God and do stupid things and make terrible mistakes."

"When it comes to perfection, God doesn't expect us to never make mistakes. Perfection for God is based upon the direction we choose for our lives."

"I need some help with that one."

"God wants us to dedicate our lives to seeking him. When we are seeking God's will, we are on target. When we choose the right course, we are perfect."

"So being perfect doesn't mean we don't make mistakes. That's amazing."

"It means that when we do make mistakes, we humble ourselves in forgiveness and genuine repentance. God does not hold our errors or sins against us. The miracle of God is that He uses imperfect people to do His perfect work."

"Flat-out amazing."

"As your brother first learned to walk, your parents beckoned him with outstretched arms. He tirelessly tried to reach them without falling down. When he did fall, your parents were never angry. They would always encourage him to get up and try again. That's how God makes us perfect—through our ongoing efforts to reach him."

Unexpectedly, the locomotive came puffing 'round the bend. Amidst the steam and noise, no surprise that Seamoor covertly caught his train.

Curiosity's Corner

Here's another place to rethink reality. Perfection points me toward my destination, not my ability to avoid error. What a radical shift in perception! All the years I've struggled to be recognized as excellent and infallible—all that misguided worry. When I pictured the child determined to walk—falling but not failing—something clicked. God is not the disapproving judge of my faults and failures. No! He opens his arms and encourages me to come to him.

More from Seamoor

Matthew 5:48

Hebrews 10:14

Romans 3:23

1 John 1:7-9

2 Corinthians 3:18

Week Sixteen

Changing Direction

"The truth has a time to its telling."

Changing Direction

Seamoor was smiling as Curiosity approached him. The men exchanged nods.

"What's on your mind?"

"I'm thinking about how much time we spend trying to make people change."

"Why is that humorous?"

"I'm grinning because I'm thinking about all the ways people try to force other people to do things against their will. It's virtually impossible to get people to change their pattern of thinking unless you change their perspective."

"Change their perspective on what?"

"On the meaning of life."

"That could take some time."

"You can say that again. People invest everything they value into their belief systems. The cost of changing how one thinks is astronomical."

"Well that's more than I can afford."

"So how are we going to change a mind?"

"Education?"

"That's how we normally attempt it."

"Is there a better way?"

"I'd like to think experience is more effective than academics. If our educational process uses experiential behavior, then I'm all for it."

"It's not that I love school. I used to get bored and fall asleep in class. But what's wrong with the classroom?"

"Most classrooms tend to be sterile. They aren't organic. Ideas are batted about and papers are written and scored. But there is something priceless about getting involved with life."

"What would that be?"

"That would be setting our goals."

"Tell me more."

"You can't change where someone is; but you can change where they're heading."

"That's a different approach."

"Changing where someone is usually meets major resistance. Such a challenge is heard as criticism. To the listener, it presumes something must be wrong. Even if the person communicating is on target, we don't like to hear it and we push back."

"So how are we going to get them to listen?"

"By painting a picture of where people want to be. We all want to make the proper decisions that ultimately lead to achieving success."

"So you are defining success as living a life that fulfills our purpose."

"Couldn't have said it any better myself. Most astute of you."

"Go on."

"And the key to fulfilling that purpose is having the confidence we've made the right choices."

"That's big."

"I'll do you one better. It's not only big, it's why we know that God's plans for us are always better than our own."

"I love it."

"In the book of Jeremiah God says, *'For I know the plans I have for you,' declares the Lord, 'plans to prosper you and not to harm you, plans to give you hope and a future.'*"

"That's great."

"We like to envision ourselves as winners. Winners live life with a clearly defined purpose. If we haven't figured out our purpose, we won't have a sense of fulfillment or achievement."

"I'm tracking with you."

"Our purpose is best defined when we see someone who achieves a worthwhile goal. How do you feel when you have accomplished your goals?"

"I feel great."

"How do you feel if you don't achieve what you want?"

"Lousy."

"Let's paint a better picture that contrasts the results of our past failed behavior versus a highly preferable view of a successful individual.

"I like what I'm hearing."

"Establishing achievable goals with a pathway that places our needs within reach gives people the willingness to make the needed shift."

"I can see that working."

"We know too much about failure. Failing to edify people when we communicate seldom results in what we want. Pushing our own agenda means we force our desires onto others. Thus, our suggestions for change lead to a major battle of the wills."

"I've been in some nasty battles myself. It can be tough convincing folks to take a different look at things."

"I consider it an art form. It takes both caring and creativity to reach people who are having a tough time."

"Yeah. When folks are hurting, they need a whole lot of love."

"I agree. The time to tell people about God's love needs to be chosen with much sensitivity. Sometimes the thing we want the most must be held back until we are ready to receive it."

"That's wisdom."

"The truth has a time to its telling."

"Now you're talking."

"King Solomon taught us that to everything there is a season. We've got to be careful about what to say as well as when to say things so we don't hurt people."

The train whistle blew. Curiosity could only shake his head and smile. This man Seamoor was such a delight and an inspiration. Two birds zipped past the pupil's head and circled around the prophet. Chattering, they rose into the sky. When Curiosity looked back down, the pathway was clear.

Curiosity's Corner

Talking with Seamoor is like target practice. Every time he says something, it takes me closer to the place I want to be. He has this approach to life that allows people to choose their own route while showing them there is a better way. He doesn't step on my toes if I think differently. My choices are made freely. We don't argue, we just kick around the most difficult subjects and watch how God leads us.

More from Seamoor

Proverbs 1:1-33

Proverbs 20:5

Philippians 3:12-14

2 Timothy 4:2

Ecclesiastes 12:13-14

Week Seventeen

Potential

"Just tell me what you see."

Potential

Curiosity noticed Seamoor was on his feet. He had a faraway look on his face. He smiled as the younger approached.

"What does the world look like from where you stand?"

"**That's quite a big question. From where I stand, or if you will, from my perspective, I look for potential.**"

"Explain."

"**Most folks don't accomplish nearly what they could.**"

"That's an understatement."

"*Yeshua* **did it all in three years.**"

"Yeah, but didn't he have thirty years to get ready?"

"**We know that, but think of how he used those thirty years. By the time he was twelve he was already teaching the elders in the temple.**"

"That would have been something to see."

"**Consider all our lost time. How much of our lives do you think are genuinely productive?**"

"I hate to think of that. It will get me depressed."

"**How much time have we wasted following paths that lead to nowhere?**"

"Aww, come on. You're not making this any easier."

"**Well, I've got some good news.**"

"What's that?"

"**There is no time that is more productive than following

God. Once you get on that path, your life has meaning. You will be accomplishing things that last into eternity."

"That's a refreshing idea."

"There's something indescribably satisfying about doing the right thing."

"You can say that again."

"All the time we spend before we recognize who *Yeshua* is, simply prepares us for what he calls us to do once we decide to follow him."

"That's looking on the bright side of things."

"Well, that's what I call recognizing our true potential."

"Yeah. I wouldn't want to miss out on my purpose."

"People who don't know the Lord do exactly that. They miss their potential for knowing God; for serving God; for building a legacy of love."

"God wants us to build a legacy of love?"

"Yes."

"That's a beautiful thought."

"I'd like to ask you the same question. What do things look like from your perspective?"

"I don't have as positive a view as you do."

"Don't compare yourself to me. Just tell me what you see."

"I see a world full of confused people. I see people trying to fit in so they'll be accepted. I see a lot of good being done, but more and more fear interfering."

"I think that's what God sees."

"Really?"

"Yes, really. One of the reasons God sent his Son was to help us know what we are supposed to be doing with ourselves."

"That's a tall order."

"Can you think of a better use of your time?"

"Frankly, no."

"There are three phases to a fulfilled life."

"Please, tell me what they are."

"First is to discover the reality of God."

"I'm with you. Surprising how many people aren't looking for God."

"Second is to accept that God is real and that He sent his Son *Yeshua* to save our souls by setting us free from the snare of sin."

"I know *Yeshua* is truly God's gift to us. I don't know how I could ever stop thanking him."

"And third, to find out whatever God asks us to do, and to do it."

"That simplifies things."

"What God asks for and expects is not difficult. Our resistance to following his plan and substituting our own ideas is where we get off track."

"Seems to me, most people either want to lead or to follow a strong leader who knows where he or she is going."

"Right you are. So the question is, 'How do you determine if the person you choose to follow is following God?'"

"Yeah. I always hear about what religious leaders claim to be doing in the name of God. Much of the time it sounds manipulative and controlling."

"That's the first clue as to whether we are dealing with God's love or humanity's desire to control. When people gain power, you soon discover what motivates them. Far too often our leaders are corrupted before they start to lead. Once they gain access to power we see what really makes them tick."

"It's in the headlines every day. I can't believe how many people are willing to cheat and lie."

"That also tells you how broken humanity is. We can't make this happen without the love of God."

The familiar chug-a-chug, punctuated by a shrill report from a steam whistle intervened.

"I'm glad God's in control and not me."

"That makes two of us."

Thinking he heard Seamoor's voice behind him, Curiosity turned. He was just in time to catch a quick glimpse of a man stepping behind a tree. Looking back to the park bench, his faithful friend was nowhere to be found.

Curiosity's Corner

Is it really that easy to boil life down to three stages? Discover God. Accept Yeshua. Find your pathway to follow. How much living does a person have to do before he can stand back and summarize the whole shooting match? The amazing part of this is that I think Seamoor has it pegged. What I like most is that he's not taking credit for all the wisdom he possesses. I want to discover my destiny's pathway.

More from Seamoor

Philippians 4:13

Matthew 6:19-21

Psalm 90:12

Psalm 34:1-3

1 Samuel 15:22

Week Eighteen

Walls

"The world judges our decision."

Walls

Seamoor sat with his hands clasped. Curiosity was full of his usual inquiries.

"You say that *Yeshua* already brought peace. How did he bring peace?"

"By conquering our enemy."

"What enemy?"

"He tore down the walls that stood between people."

"What do you mean by 'walls'?"

"What stands between people is fear and fanaticism, injustice and jealousy, disillusionment and deceit. The list continues. When we are looking for reasons not to trust, we are divided. Our enemy builds walls that stand between humanity and peace."

"I get it. That's a sad testimony concerning humankind's condition."

"Sad but true. On the other hand, we have new life. We now enjoy an extraordinary list of God's blessings for harmony and healing, hope and holiness, harvest and Heaven."

"Now we're talking! When God gave Moses the Torah, didn't that solve humankind's problems? Wasn't that God's intention?"

"It wasn't that the Law failed to show us what God wanted us to do. The Torah reveals that we can't earn salvation without him. The law we thought would set us free actually convicted us of our sinful status."

"How did that happen?"

"When Jews tried to live under the requirements of the law, they soon realized only a perfect person could fulfill the Torah. They knew no one was perfect. They hoped following the letter of the law as closely as possible would elevate their standing with God. Unfortunately, that means our relationship with God would be subject to human control."

"So you're telling me it took a perfect man to be the perfect sacrifice?"

"Precisely. The Torah points us toward living a sinless life to fulfill its ordinances. Only an unblemished human sacrifice could offer total forgiveness for humanity's flaws. *Yeshua* fulfills every requirement—including the sacrifice of his own life as an atonement for our souls."

"So if *Yeshua* overcame all our shortcomings through his sacrifice, why hasn't he broken through into our lives today? What are we doing wrong?"

"In a word, 'honor.' We haven't honored our Messiah."

"That's pretty clear. But I'm sure you've noticed that the people who honor *Yeshua* today are frowned upon."

"It's almost always been this way. There's a price to pay. *Yeshua* paid for our salvation. But he had a high purpose and calling. He exemplified the fact that all of us have to overcome sin to honor God. That sets believers apart from the rest of the world. The world judges our decision."

"So it takes guts to be a believer."

"Following *Yeshua* is not for the faint of heart. The most common phrase in the Bible is, *'Fear not.'*"

"Really?"

"People don't know how to properly relate to the realm of the Spirit without the power of God. So our enemy, who is very cunning and who's been at this for a long time, finds our weaknesses to defeat us."

"You are making me rethink history. It appears we have been fighting this battle for a long time."

"Yep. Ever since the Garden of Eden."

"All the way back to the beginning."

"Of course, there are notable periods of time when the children of God have found favor. There's much inspiring history on outpourings, revivals, renewals, and awakenings, but only for limited seasons."

"What's God waiting for?"

"Occasionally God gives us a taste of his goodness to remind us of his plans for our future. But he has a grand finale up his sleeve."

"Only God could come up with a design as vast as that. None of us live long enough to think on such a broad scale."

"And only God could fulfill it to the letter. When the Bible was given to man, it did more than give us rules to live by."

"What do you mean?"

"The Holy Scriptures are recorded by prophets inspired by the Spirit of God. Often they would foretell the future. There are prophecies that span thousands of years. The great majority of those promises have already been fulfilled."

"No kidding. The Bible covers past, present, and future?"

"In every dimension."

"What prophecies haven't been fulfilled?"

"Those remaining are mostly end-times prophecies. They give us a glimpse into what must occur before the Second Coming. The next awakening won't end until our *King Yeshua* returns to reign in glory."

"The Second Coming?"

"Yes. *Yeshua* is coming back."

"Hold the presses. You really believe he's coming back?"

"Yes."

"In the flesh?"

"That's what the good book says."

A low-rolling thunder accompanied the shrill blast from the train today. Curiosity took in all the sounds. A smile came over his face. He looked up into the sunlight. Things were different now. He waved good-bye to Seamoor.

Curiosity's Corner

I'm getting a lesson about inside out thoughts. My views on law are being reformulated right in front of my eyes. This is taking me out of my comfort zone. I thought the law was for our protection. Now I'm learning that God gave Moses the law so we would be able to recognize our sin, realize we can't live a proper life without God, turn to him and surrender daily until the Second Coming. Come on!

More from Seamoor

Genesis 12:1-3

John 10:10-11

Joshua 6:5

2 Timothy 3:16-17

Revelation 1:7-8

Week Nineteen

Joy

"How about a double portion?"

Joy

Seamoor was in a playful mood. His hat was tipped funny as he scrunched up his nose when Curiosity sat down.

"What's got into you?"

"Some folks call it the joy of the Lord."

"What's that?"

"That's when the Spirit of God makes you feel wonderful, full of life, and overwhelmed by a radiant sense of well-being."

"I'll take some of that."

"How about a double portion? That's biblical."

Curiosity started to giggle. Seamoor made a face and Curiosity fell on the ground and started rolling around with hysterical belly laughs.

"Be careful what you ask for!"

That remark sent Curiosity into shrieks of laughter. He pointed at Seamoor, but was at a loss for words.

"Are you starting to get a taste of God's love for you?"

Curiosity wailed with delight.

"Can you bottle this stuff?"

"Of course, but what would you say on the warning label?"

"Oh, that's good!"

Curiosity was now on his hands and knees just trying to catch his breath. Seamoor was leaning over on the bench holding his head in his hands.

"I don't want to stop laughing."

"Why would you?"

"I can't imagine."

"I hear tell you've got quite an imagination, Mr. Curiosity."

"You hear? You hear what? Who told you?"

"**A little birdie told me so.**"

And wouldn't you know it? A bird swooped down and landed on the back of the park bench and started twittering. Seamoor glanced at the bird, then back at Curiosity and smirked. Tears of joy welled up in Curiosity's eyes.

"How did you manage to do that?"

"**That wasn't me.**"

"This bird is no accident."

"**No, he isn't.**"

Seamoor returned his gaze to the winged messenger and spoke. The bird tweeted.

"**You don't say!**"

"What the…?"

Seamoor continued his dialogue with his feathered friend.

"**So what do you want me to tell him?**"

The bird whistled again.

"**He already knows that.**"

The bird took flight and was gone. Curiosity was awestruck. Seamoor looked back at him.

"What did the bird say?"

"**He said, 'It's a wonderful day.'**"

"Aww, come on. How do you know what he said?"

"**What do you mean? It was easy to understand.**"

"Huh? I suppose you know the language."

"**In fact I do.**"

"Right. What language was he speaking?"

"**He was speaking Bird-cha-Geese.**"

Curiosity stopped for a second, then repeated the phrase. "Bird-cha-Geese."

This time he howled with laughter. He rolled over on the ground onto his back with his knees up to his chest in the fetal position.

"I give up. You win."

"**Don't tell me, tell the bird.**"

"I can't even breathe. How am I going to tell the bird?"

"You can always Twitter him."

Curiosity started gasping with joy. He was a puddle of mirth rolling on the lawn. Seamoor was overcome with gladness. Contentment reigned down on them both.

"I don't ever want to go back to being normal again."

"Why not make this the new normal?"

"Sign me up."

"Philippians 4 tells us, *'Rejoice in the Lord always—again I will say, rejoice!'*"

"I can't remember the last time I've laughed so hard."

"I can't help but notice how often folks decide that believers have to be upset about something. They think we don't have a good time."

"Well they missed the boat on that idea."

"For some reason people don't believe God has a sense of humor. They put him way up there in Heaven, far, far away from us. They think he's angry all the time. They think he likes wielding all his power and showing his might by sending down lightning bolts and creating natural disasters for a pastime. They believe God gets his joy by making us feel small and insignificant."

"That's not a pretty picture of the One who loves us so much He would send *Yeshua* to make a way for us to spend eternity with him."

"You know, God didn't go to all this trouble to make this planet and put us here so we would sound like sour grapes."

"We could always make sour grape juice!"

Now it was Seamoor's opportunity to get the giggles.

"That's what happens if you don't wash your feet before you step on the grapes. Maybe that's how God made his grapes of wrath."

"You have a very juicy sense of humor."

"Don't press me."

Unable to breathe for all the joy and laughter, Curiosity holds up his hands in surrender mode.

"I give. Mercy. I surrender."

The soft steady sound of the oncoming train carried through the trees. Seamoor stood up and wiped his brow. Grinning, he set off for his destination.

"I have 'smiles' to go before I sleep."

Curiosity's Corner

Freedom! I have never laughed so hard in all my life. My guts are sore from an uninhibited joy I have always hoped for. God, I feel so good. All I can do is thank you. You have tapped into some part of me that has been longing for release. Today I found it. For anyone who thinks believing in God is for dull, uptight folks without a sense of humor, have I got news for you!

More from Seamoor

Nehemiah 8:10

Psalm 70:4

Job 8:21

Acts 2:28

Proverbs 17:22

Week Twenty

One New Man

"We won't find it without God."

One New Man

Seamoor was watching the clouds sail by and humming a tune when Curiosity caught up with him. Both were in a good mood and exchanged greetings.

"How are you today?"

"Just fine, and you?"

"I'm doing quite well, thanks."

"What's on your mind?"

"The reason I first decided to meet you is because my friends told me you advised them that the pathway to peace had already been paved."

"Your friends are being more than gracious with that description."

"Nevertheless, you told them that the One New Man was the answer."

"True."

"So just where do I find this One New Man?"

"You'll be delighted to know you have already met him."

"What do you mean?"

"You know who he is."

"OK. I give up. Give me a hint."

"You see him every day."

"Where?"

"In the mirror!"

"What?"

"If you're looking for the One New Man, you've already met him."

"I don't get it."

"**One New Man is an identity given to us by God. When you accept *Yeshua* as Lord and Savior, you're grafted into his body of believers. Our faith in God unites us both to God and to one another. The book of Ephesians declares we are "*One New Man.*" We are connected for eternity.**"

"So all believers are now united as One New Man."

"**That's what I've been saying.**"

"Now that's a revelation!"

"**God says the uniting of Jews and Gentiles creates a brand-new identity and that is the One New Man.**"

"That's remarkable. You're telling me that when we accept *Yeshua* as Lord and Savior that the problems between different people—even people from differing races and cultures who violently disagree—have been solved?"

"**That's about it.**"

"Just what did *Yeshua* do that made this possible?"

"**When *Yeshua* died on the cross, he died for humanity to be restored into proper relationship with God.**"

"Go on."

"**The scourging he endured and the blood he shed wasn't for *Yeshua's* sin—he had no sin. So if He had no sin, whose sin is it?**"

"Wow. Now I see. It's my sin. He died for all our sins."

"**Our sin stood between us and God. Because God is pure and holy, He needs us to be made clean so we can stand before him.**"

"Unbelievable!"

"**Actually, it's quite believable.**"

"I stand corrected."

"**The wall that separated all ethnicities was destroyed on the cross.**"

"This is front page news."

"**It's no accident the events of a small nation named Israel are splashed across the headlines most every day.**"

"It's like God doesn't want us to forget about Israel."

"No, He definitely does not."

"All of a sudden this makes sense. Everybody fights for control of Jerusalem. God wants us to love Jerusalem, not fight over it. That's where it all began."

"And that's where it will all end."

"Full circle."

"Full circle."

"I've heard people talk about a massive battle over Israel during end-times."

"It will be a conflict that will stagger the imagination."

"So what's all this talk about world peace if we just end up hurting and killing each other?"

"World peace won't be a reality before *Yeshua* returns in all His Glory."

"I must have missed something major. How do we find peace?"

"We won't find it without God."

"I can see that. But how does the One New Man fit into all of this?

"Remember I said the One New Man is an identity. Within that identity—all who believe make up the body of Messiah—therein is the place of peace."

"Please explain some more."

"We find our peace through our identity as One New Man."

"That makes perfect sense."

"You are the One New Man."

"Wait, you're telling me that the person I've been looking for is me?"

"That's right! Your search is over."

"So the person who God calls to be his peacemaker is the One New Man."

"That's what the Good Book says."

"And that One New Man is me."

"Now you've got it."

"So it's up to me to make peace."
"Precisely."
"I'm not sure if I'm qualified."
"Why not?"
"I never tried to figure out how to make peace before."
"You don't have to."
"Hold on a minute. You just finished convincing me that because I believe that *Yeshua* is the Messiah that I am part of his body."
"Affirmative."
"Therefore, whether Jew or Gentile, both are identified as One New Man."
"Correct."
"I have to think about this."
"I expect you will. While you're at it, pray for the peace of Jerusalem."

Seamoor raised his hands toward Heaven, blessing God. Curiosity never heard the whistle that day, as he was lost in thought.

Curiosity's Corner

It's taken me the whole semester to get back to the question I first wanted Seamoor to answer, "How do we attain world peace?" Wouldn't you know it, the answer I'm getting from my buddy is that it's up to me. I'm equally thrilled and dismayed. I love seeing I can make the difference. I also shudder at the idea that I'm supposed to have enough wisdom and faith to tell people about the One New Man.

More from Seamoor

2 Corinthians 5:17

Colossians 3:10

Romans 6:6

Jeremiah 30

Psalm 122:6

Week Twenty-one

Godly Government

"God blesses His followers."

Godly Government

Upon greeting, Curiosity and Seamoor hugged like old friends.

"What does unity look like?"

"Unity happens when others become more important than myself."

"That's a tall order. Has any society ever behaved that way?"

"Yes, we do have record of one."

"Interesting. Let me guess. Is it communist or socialist?"

"No."

"What's wrong with either of those?"

"First, following *Yeshua* will improve whatever system we live under. Second, for all their high-minded rhetoric, every form of government that claims equality comes under the auspices of a ruling class or a specialized group of leaders. There is a common fallacy that has affected our thinking that peace is inevitable if everyone gets treated the same."

"So it's the opportunity that determines equality, not the other way around, such as when a government claims its policy creates equality."

"You got it. Excellent insight. A government's rulership of its citizens is not what creates equality, but that's what leaders like to claim. It's equitably granting citizens the best opportunity to express their own gifts and talents that creates genuine equality. The government serves the people, not the other way around."

"So when and where was there a time when people made others more important than themselves?"

"**The first century church was perhaps the most unselfish culture in the history of our planet. The followers of *Yeshua* saw what life was like in the kingdom and embraced it. They sold their assets and laid the proceeds at the apostles' feet to share as they saw fit to help all in need.**"

"You're kidding me."

"**No, I'm not. It's true.**"

"How come I never heard about that?"

"**There's a lot in this book that the world doesn't know about. The Holy Scriptures teach us the way to have peace, but we haven't bothered to put it into action. The world is a skeptical place.**"

"I've noticed. It's sad."

"**Only sad if you buy into beliefs that lack a godly foundation.**"

"How do we know that God's plan actually works?"

"**History has confirmed it over and over. God blesses His followers. As people in authority see kingdom principles working, they get to make a better choice. They may accept these principles and bless their people, or if they fear losing control, they often shut the government down.**"

"Wow. Based on world history, we have to make some serious adjustments."

"**As a governed society that may be true, but for each individual, freedom is as close as your heartfelt commitment to follow *Yeshua*.**"

"Yeah that's right. Boy, this doesn't work the way that I expected it to."

"**How many things in life do? The magnitude of genuine faith cannot be measured or contained. Faith in the Son of God moves mountains.**"

"What makes you so sure?"

"Genuine unity of faith reunites families, stymies strife, and gives us a safe place to grow. Life flows in the manner prescribed by God. There is a direct link between peace and prosperity when a nation honors its families and turns their hearts to the living God."

"This is beginning to sound like the genuine peace humanity needs."

"The godly authority that flows out of harmony and lovingkindness is unsettling to those who abuse the privilege of leadership. Such leaders fail to recognize that doing good has always been God's intention for all his children. Healthy institutions govern most effectively through public service, not by creating political servants."

"This tells me the people who are weak in their values shouldn't be placed in power. It seems to me we elect people based upon their popularity instead of their value system."

"The public presumes leaders have become popular based upon a high code of ethics. If a moral system of values has not been deeply instilled into their character before they get into the office, when they do gain power, they won't know what to do with it."

"That's very scary."

"That's the world we live in. And that has a lot to do with why this world appears to be a very scary place."

"So who in leadership can we trust?"

"I suggest we find out whom our leaders trust. If they trust in God, then God will do remarkable exploits among them."

"That sounds rather simplistic."

"Why do people insist on making God so difficult?"

"I'd guess it's because we can't see."

"Yet we see him at work daily."

Hoot. Hoot. Seamoor extended his hand to Curiosity and grasped it firmly.

"I must take my leave."
"Will I see you again?"
"I'm always nearby."
"I'll miss you, Seamoor."
"I treasure our friendship."
"Your gift is mine to receive."
Seamoor entered the fog and merged into the mist.

Curiosity's Corner

I don't know if I'll ever see Seamoor again. When he said good-bye, I could tell that he was moving on. He stepped onto that train and into another realm. His vast knowledge comes from some place beyond the confines of this planet. Why I was given the privilege of befriending him I may never know. He showed me the reality of the Kingdom of Heaven. Someday soon he and I will walk as one in glory.

More from Seamoor

Exodus 3:14

Colossians 1:16

Isaiah 9:6-7

Proverbs 3:5-6

Revelation 19

About the Author

Majestic Glory Ministries founder Robert Wolff promotes reconciliation between Jews and Gentiles by accepting our God-given identity as One New Man in our Messiah Yeshua. Robert's vision for walking out our calling incorporates a broad view of shared challenges to initiate fresh, coordinated approaches for problem solving. He seeks to achieve unity within the Kingdom of God by encouraging multicultural acts of lovingkindness and service to our communities coupled with mutually beneficial enterprises to stimulate infrastructure growth.

Robert orchestrates groundbreaking ministry outreaches worldwide, such as the *Every Tribe Every Nation* Project joining the First Nations of America with the nation of Israel by integrating available resources with agricultural expertise. He launched the O.A.T.H. Project (One Against Trafficking Humans) as a vehicle to combat slavery by unifying believers without competitive friction. He participates in a myriad of Messianic groups as he ministers in a variety of faith-based settings using Kingdom Kinetics to forge strategic partnerships.

As Executive Editor of *UNITY: Awakening the One New Man* and authoring *Catch & Release: A Church Set Free, My First 40 Days with the Lord*, and *Have You Seen the Lamb?*, he provides literary tools for spiritual growth. He earned a Bachelor's in Economics at Colorado College and a Master's of Theology from Fuller Theological Seminary, with associated studies at Oral Roberts University and The King's University. Robert and his wife Wendy reside in Malibu, California.

www.ingramcontent.com/pod-product-compliance
Lightning Source LLC
Chambersburg PA
CBHW071736080526
44588CB00013B/2051